When the Going Gets Tough

DISCOVERY SERIES BIBLE STUDY
For individuals or groups

During his years of pastoring, radio broadcasting, and serving as president of Moody Bible Institute and Cornerstone University, Joe Stowell has helped many hurting people find strength for the journey of life.

With a reassuring realism rooted in the timeless counsel of the Word of God, Joe proclaims a message of hope and faith that we can use as we travel the wonderful yet difficult road of life.

That is the kind of encouragement you will find in this adaptation of the booklet *When The Going Gets Tough*, excerpted from Dr. Stowell's book *The Upside Of Down*, which was published by Discovery House Publishers.

—*Martin R. De Haan II*
RBC Ministries

This Discovery Series Bible Study is based on
When The Going Gets Tough (HP072), one of the popular Discovery Series booklets from RBC Ministries. Find out more about the Discovery Series at www.discoveryseries.org.

Copyright © 2012 by Discovery House Publishers

Discovery House Publishers is affiliated with RBC Ministries,
Grand Rapids, Michigan

Requests for permission to quote from this book should be directed to the Permissions Department, Discovery House Publishers, PO Box 3566, Grand Rapids, MI 49501, or contact us by e-mail at permissionsdept@dhp.org

Unless otherwise indicated, Scripture is taken from the New King James Version.
©1982, Thomas Nelson, Inc. Used by permission. All rights reserved.

Managing Editor: Dave Branon
Study Guide questions: Sim Kay Tee, Dave Branon
Graphic Design: Steve Gier
Cover Photo: Terry Bidgood

ISBN: 978-1-57293-718-5
Printed in the United States of America

First printing in 2012

Table of Contents

FOREWORD: When The Going Gets Tough 1
HOW TO USE DISCOVERY SERIES BIBLE STUDIES 4
FOR DEVOTION AND **MEDITATION** 12, 22, 32, 40, 48, 56
Our Daily Bread articles about trials

1 UNDERSTANDING OUR TRIALS   6
ROLLER-COASTER RIDE / HOW TO VIEW TROUBLE / WHAT GOOD IS TROUBLE?
STUDY GUIDE 1   **10**

2 TRIALS OF LIFE (PART ONE)   13
TRIALS OF PLACE & RACE / TRIALS OF TEMPTATION / TRIALS OF IDENTIFICATION
STUDY GUIDE 2   **20**

3 TRIALS OF LIFE (PART TWO)   23
TRIALS OF DISCIPLINE / TRIALS OF CONSEQUENCES FOR SIN
STUDY GUIDE 3   **30**

4 TRIALS OF LIFE (PART THREE)   33
TRIALS OF DISPLAY / TRIALS OF BROKEN EXPECTATION
STUDY GUIDE 4   **38**

5 RESPONSES OF THE HEART (PART ONE)   41
HOW WILL WE RESPOND? / CONTROLLING OUR RESPONSE / THE RESULT
STUDY GUIDE 5   **46**

6 RESPONSES OF THE HEART (PART TWO)   49
THE JOY OF OUR RESPONSE / THE CONTENT OF OUR RESPONSE
STUDY GUIDE 6   **54**

Leader's and User's Guide   57

How To Use
DISCOVERY SERIES BIBLE STUDIES

The Purpose
The Discovery Series Bible Study (DSBS) series provides assistance to pastors and lay leaders in guiding and teaching fellow Christians with lessons adapted from RBC Ministries Discovery Series booklets and supplemented from items taken from the pages of *Our Daily Bread*. The DSBS series uses the inductive study method to help Christians understand the Bible more clearly.

The Format
READ: Each DSBS book is divided into a series of lessons. For each lesson, you will read a few pages that will give you insight into one aspect of the overall study. Included in some studies will be FOCAL POINT and TIME OUT FOR THEOLOGY segments to help you think through the material. These can be used as discussion starters for group sessions.

RESPOND: At the end of the reading is a two-page STUDY GUIDE to help participants respond to and reflect on the subject. If you are the leader of a group study, ask each member to preview the STUDY GUIDE before the group gets together. Don't feel that you have to work your way through each question in the STUDY GUIDE; let the interest level of the participants dictate the flow of the discussion. The questions are designed for either group or individual study. Here are the parts of that guide:

MEMORY VERSE: A short Scripture passage that focuses your thinking on the biblical truth at hand and can be used for memorization. You might suggest memorization as a part of each meeting.

WARMING UP: A general interest question that can foster discussion (group) or contemplation (individual).

THINKING THROUGH: Questions that will help a group or a student interact with the reading. These questions help drive home the critical concepts of the book.

DIGGING IN: An inductive study of a related passage of Scripture, reminding the group or the student of the importance of Scripture as the final authority.

GOING FURTHER: A two-part wrap-up of the response: REFER suggests ways to compare the ideas of the lesson with teachings in other parts of the Bible. REFLECT challenges the group or the learner to apply the teaching in real life.

OUR DAILY BREAD: After each STUDY GUIDE session will be an *Our Daily Bread* article that relates to the topic. You can use this for further reflection or for an introduction to a time of prayer.

Go to the Leader's and User's Guide on page 57 for further suggestions about using the Discovery Series Bible Study.

1

Understanding Our Trials

Roller-Coaster Ride

Getting through a season of trouble is a lot like surviving a roller-coaster ride—except that we do not volunteer for trouble, and trouble was never intended to be fun.

Trouble is filled with stomach-wrenching drops, dips, and sudden curves. And just when we think we've caught our breath, we're dropping again.

If we didn't know better, we might think that this roller-coaster ride is a random experience—that somehow the forces that lift us up and push us down are whims of fate.

Thankfully, it's not a random ride at all. Those who understand the work of God in and through our troubles know that He does not abandon us to disaster. Rather, with all the strength of His character, He provides a well-engineered superstructure that supports the process along a carefully planned set of tracks and guardrails. Even when the ride is too hectic, unsettling, and twisted for us to sense the presence of His support and guidance, it's still there. Our only hope in it all is to stay in the car and find something solid to hold on to through every turn of the experience.

When trouble invades our comfort zones, two needs rise to the top: the need for understanding (to find answers to the probing and disturbing questions that crowd our minds and souls) **and the need for healing** (to feel better and to finish the problem). Of the two, **understanding is the key** to managing the problem effectively to its ultimate outcome. Without the understanding that produces the right answers, there is no sense of direction and no hope in which to feel secure.

How To View Trouble

The apostle James used a specific word for *trouble* that leads to a helpful understanding of what trouble is. The essence of this word led J. B. Phillips to paraphrase James 1:2 by saying that when troubles come, "Don't resent them as intruders, but welcome them as friends!"

When James wrote, "Consider it all joy, my brethren, when you encounter various trials" (James 1:2 NASB), his choice of words was strategic. The Greek word for *trial* is a word that means "to examine or test for the purpose of proving or revealing something about the thing tested." **Trial, then, is "a test that reveals something for a specific purpose."**

Of all the things we could say about trials—that they are disappointing, discouraging, humiliating, uncomfortable, painful, and disheartening—God sees them, among other reasons, as tests that reveal our true selves. It's a sure thing that in trouble, the real me becomes apparent quickly. **Trouble is revelatory.**

Trouble is one of God's ways of examining our lives. When we are on "Easy Street"—and thank the Lord that He lets us come up for air periodically—it is hard to know what we are really like. We can carry on a cosmetic existence and fool ourselves, and most people, about our true nature.

But when trouble hits our lives, what we are really like is quickly revealed. Trouble shows our friends, our spouses, our children, and our acquaintances what we are like. Even more unsettling, it forces us to start seeing ourselves for what we really are.

> ### ■ FOCAL POINT
> Stowell suggests that "trouble is revelatory;" that is, it reveals our "true selves." Can you think of a time when trouble revealed a "true you" that you didn't like?

I am committed to the sanctification process in my life, to becoming increasingly pure as I grow in my walk with God. Yet sanctification is tough, even in situations that are not life threatening.

Several years ago, when my son was a student playing basketball, it was a trial to see him sitting on the bench when he should have been playing. A small trial, but a revealing one. Worse yet was what it was like when he got into the game and the referee started to harass him. As I rose out of my seat, I began to "express myself," only to feel my wife tug at my coat: "Joe, you're the president of Moody Bible Institute," she would remind me. There is much in me that needs to be worked on. More important than the "obvious lack of judgment by the coach or the referee" was my lack of maturity in terms of self-control and Christlikeness. The pressure of the "trial" during the game gave me a good look at myself and showed me areas in which I needed to grow.

Without that strategic perspective, we tend to focus on the external aspects of our problems. Yet if we keep in mind that trouble is in part intended to reveal the "real me" in each of us so we can grow, our focus in pain will move from pity to the production of God's glory in and through us.

 What Good Is Trouble?

Among other things, **trouble reveals where I am in the growth process** in terms of my conformity to the image and character of Christ. It gets me beyond assumptions to reality. Am I a forgiving person? Am I kind? Understanding? Just? Loving? Helpful? Patient? Or am I angry, slanderous, self-centered, inflexible, manipulative, weak, and ill-equipped to respond to trials correctly?

It is helpful to see ourselves as we really are. Trouble reveals that, and it turns the agenda toward the things in our lives that need to be changed so we can grow to be more like Him—and that, of course, is the purpose of our redemption (Romans 8:28–29) and one of God's purposes in trials (James 1:2–4).

William Coltman was pastor of Highland Park Baptist Church in Detroit, Michigan, for more than forty years. He served with dignity through many difficult times. At one point in his life he was falsely accused of moral indiscretion, and his wife refused to go to church with him. Each Sunday she left the house to attend another church down the street.

His secretary of many years told me that through it all she "never heard him say a negative word about anyone!" In the test, his character was revealed and Christ was glorified.

> ### ■ FOCAL POINT
> What are a couple of things that—because of specific trials—you discovered that you should change in your life?

What are trials anyway? Often they are tests to let us know where we are in the process of growing up in Him.

James 1:2 goes on to qualify the nature of these tests by saying that "many kinds" of trials will enter our lives. Knowing what kind of trouble to expect is a great help in being ready to meet that trouble.

The Scripture speaks of at least seven different kinds of trouble, which we will examine in this study.

1 Understanding Our Trials

STUDY GUIDE
read pages 6–9

To begin to sense the best way to respond when trouble comes our way.

MEMORY VERSE
1 Peter 1:6—
"In this you greatly rejoice, though now for a little while, if need be, you have been grieved by various trials."

Warming Up

Think about the most troubling trials in your life recently. Do you agree that "trouble is a lot like surviving a roller-coaster ride"? If so, what part of the ride are you on right now? Going up? Going down? Twisting? Scared of crashing?

Thinking Through

1. On pages 6–7, Joe Stowell says that God provides "a well-engineered superstructure that supports the process." What do you see as the superstructure of your life that helps you when you face trouble?

2. When trouble comes and you have "the need for understanding" and the "need for healing," to whom do you usually turn?

3. If trouble reveals where you are in the growing process, what have your hard times revealed about you?

Going Further

Refer

Look at these passages that mention trouble. Who is mentioning the trouble, what is the problem experienced, and what is the outcome?
Psalm 6:3
Lamentations 1:20
Acts 20:19–23

Digging In   Read   1 Peter 1:5–9

1. According to verse 5 of 1 Peter 1, what is the characteristic that seems to be the prerequisite for the rejoicing in verse 6?

2. If you remain faithful during trials, what will be tested according to verse 7? After it is tested, what will be the good results of the "genuineness of your faith"?

3. Those of us who never saw Jesus, the object of our faith, are singled out in verse 8. What is the positive result of our faith?

> [5] [You] are kept by the power of God through faith for salvation ready to be revealed in the last time. [6] In this you greatly rejoice, though now for a little while, if need be, you have been grieved by various trials, [7] that the genuineness of your faith, being much more precious than gold that perishes, though it is tested by fire, may be found to praise, honor, and glory at the revelation of Jesus Christ, [8] whom having not seen you love. Though now you do not see Him, yet believing, you rejoice with joy inexpressible and full of glory, [9] receiving the end of your faith—the salvation of your souls.

Prayer Time

Use the *Our Daily Bread* article on the next page as a guide for a devotional and prayer time relating to the topic of trials.

Reflect

Do you see the trials in your life as punishment, or do you see them, as Joe Stowell says on page 9, "as tests to let us know where we are in the process of growing up in Him"?

What good have you noticed that has come from the trouble you've had to go through?

Our Daily Bread: For reflection & meditation about **trials**

A Good Miss

I was watching with interest a game in which my grandson Peter was playing. It was his second year of playing T-ball, which introduces six-year-olds to baseball. In this game the ball is placed on a rubber post that sits on homeplate. A baseball rests on top of the batting tee just waiting to be slugged. The youngsters swing with all their might, hoping to hit a home run, but often they miss the ball completely.

This had just happened to my grandson, and he appeared to be very upset with himself. The coach wanted to encourage him, so he shouted, "That was a good miss, Peter!" My grandson had missed, yet the coach called it "good."

This reminds me of our failures as believers in Christ. God never calls our sin good, yet He doesn't treat failure as final. By His grace, He can bring good out of our greatest defeat. In Romans 8:28 we read that God is working all things together for the good of those who love Him. What a hopeful mystery!

If you love God and want to please Him, don't give up or get down on yourself. Ask Him for forgiveness and for strength to overcome your weaknesses. Trust Him. Let Him bring "good" out of your miss.

—*Dennis De Haan*

ROMANS 8:28—
We know that all things work together for good to those who love God.

■ Read today's *Our Daily Bread* at **www.rbc.org/odb**

Trials of Life

PART ONE

Trials Of Place And Race

First, and probably most common, are trials of place and race. Scripture affirms that we live in a fallen place. This planet is under the rule of our adversary, Satan. Earth is his domain. In 2 Corinthians, Paul calls him "the god of this age" (4:4). We are also part of a fallen race. Again, Paul explains this for us when he says, "just as through one man sin entered the world, and death through sin, and thus spread death to all men" (Romans 5:12). Apart from the help of God, all of us are prone to express our fallenness in many kinds of damaging ways.

We can count on it—living in a fallen place and being a part of a fallen race is going to produce difficult times. Originally, this place was a perfect environment where productive work, fellowship with God, and morally responsible actions provided fulfillment and unhindered joy. But in Genesis 3, sin entered the picture and messed up the scene. The rest of Scripture speaks to the struggle of real people trying to live in a fallen place as part of a fallen race.

The wonderful thing about the scope of biblical history is that whereas it starts with a perfect creation and then records the Fall, it ends with the glorious consummation of all things. One of my all-time favorite passages in Scripture is in Revelation: "The former things are passed away. . . . Behold, I make all things new" (Revelation 21:4–5 KJV). What a great hope for us! In that new environment there will be no more death, no more tears, no more sorrow, no more pain, no more crying. Until then, though, we are a fallen race planted in a fallen place.

When we were children, we played the game "So Big." We couldn't wait to grow up. Then we became teenagers. We looked in the mirror and said, "No

■ FOCAL POINT

The greatest sermons I have ever heard were not preached from pulpits, but from sickbeds. The greatest, deepest truths of God's Word have often been revealed . . . by humble souls who have gone through the seminary of affliction and have learned experientially the deep things of the ways of God.

Are you afflicted and suffering, precious child of God? Then remember—your Father still knows best . . . We may not know what God is doing now, but someday we shall understand and be like Him.

—Dr. M. R. De Haan
Broken Things

way! That can't be my body!" Our faces erupted like volcanoes, we started to become men and women, and we didn't like what was happening to us. Then we reached our thirties, and our bodies began to slow down. We spent vast sums of money at health spas. Our bodies sagged and wrinkled, and we started looking for the plastic surgeon.

We look forward to retirement, but our bodies will retire before we do. Our back goes out more often than we do. When we lean down to pick something up, we want to stay down to see how many other things we can get while we're there.

Our bodies get sick—and rarely on schedule. Some of us live in bodies that are diseased. Arthritis, diabetes, and Alzheimer's disease plague many. Death stands ready to rob us of those we love in untimely and unsettling ways. It's a fallen place, and we're a fallen race. Trouble comes with the territory.

Fallen people use, manipulate, and abuse us. Horrific accidents, killer tornadoes, and devastating earthquakes disrupt our lives. It's all part of being planted on a planet damaged by the rule of Satan and sin.

When a trial of place and race impacts our lives, what ought to be revealed? In 2 Corinthians 12, Paul valiantly struggles with his thorn in the flesh. He prays three times that God will remove it from him. But it's clear that it's not God's will that the thorn should be removed. It has purpose. So Paul acknowledges the thorn's presence and recognizes that it has purpose, which is to keep him from becoming conceited because of the grand revelations God gave him (12:7). He submits to the trial without bitterness or blaming God, and he claims that through his weakness God will make him strong (v. 9).

Trials Of Temptation

The second kind of trial we find in Scripture is the trial of temptation. In Matthew 4:1 we read, "Then Jesus was led by the Spirit into the wilderness to be tempted by the devil." Interestingly enough, the same Greek word sometimes translated as the word *trial* is translated here as the word *tempted*. Satan led Christ through the temptation of the pride of life and the lust of the flesh. He hit Christ at every vulnerable point we struggle with as humans. The Lord countered His trouble at every point by a response from Scripture that kept Him unflinchingly loyal to God.

Temptation is unavoidable. It intrudes into the life of the businessman on the road, the homemaker in her house, the citizen filling out income tax forms, and the person who has been hurt by others. We feel the temptation to strike out in revenge, to gossip, or to slander. These are significant temptations.

I have a friend in the ministry who, after checking into his hotel, got on the elevator with two attractive young women. As the door closed, one of them said, "Hey, how about a little fun with us tonight?"

He thought to himself, *Who would know?*

My friend later told me, "It was like God pulled a curtain down in front of me, and on the curtain was Galatians 6:8, 'The one who sows to please his sinful nature, from that nature will reap destruction' " (NIV). He said no to the women and yes to God. His relationship to God was more important than the seductive pleasure of sin.

When I was a little boy, someone wrote in my Bible, "This book will keep you from sin, or sin will keep you from this book." In the face of troubling temptation, the power of God's Word is an indispensable ally. As the psalmist said, "Thy word have I hid in mine heart, that I might not sin against Thee" (Psalm 119:11 KJV).

Trials Of Identification

A third kind of trial that we can expect is the test of identification. In chapters 15 and 17 of John's gospel, Jesus told His disciples that they could expect the world to be rough on them, as it had been on Him. They could expect to be thrown out of the synagogue, to be disowned by their families, and in some cases even to be murdered—all because they bore His name and were identified with His cause.

History records that because the early church broke bread at Communion and said, "This is the body of Christ," the culture of that day accused them of cannibalism. Christians claimed Communion as their love feast, and the culture of that day accused them of improprieties in those private observances. In the midst of this pressure, Peter encouraged the believers to persevere. He wrote to a suffering church, "Live such good lives among the pagans that, though they accuse you of doing wrong, they may see your good deeds and glorify God on the day he visits us" (1 Peter 2:12 NIV). He added:

> ### ■ FOCAL POINT
>
> Think about the difference in the results of giving in to temptation vs. the results of resisting temptation. After giving in, what negative consequences follow? After resisting, what positive consequences follow?

How is it to your credit if you receive a beating for doing wrong and endure it? But if you suffer for doing good and you endure it, this is commendable before God. To this you were called, because Christ suffered for you, leaving you an example, that you should follow in his steps. "He committed no sin, and no deceit was found in his mouth." When they hurled their insults at him, he did not retaliate; when he suffered, he made no threats. Instead, he entrusted himself to him who judges justly. He himself bore our sins in his body on the tree, so that we might die to sins and live for righteousness; by his wounds you have been healed (vv. 20–24 NIV).

As the world becomes more secularized, we can expect trouble in an environment increasingly hostile toward the values of righteousness we hold dear. Now more than ever, we as God's people must be prepared to pass the test of trials that come because of our identification with Christ.

Dennis was on the fast track upward with Cox newspapers, headquartered in Atlanta, Georgia. He had been the publisher of the *Springfield News-Sun* in Springfield, Ohio, and had served Cox as the publisher of the *Dayton Daily News* in Dayton, Ohio. In both settings, he had made the newspapers he managed

> ### ■ FOCAL POINT
> What erroneous ideas do non-Christians that you know have about Christians? Are these the fault of the way we conduct ourselves or are they the result of misconceptions of the non-Christians?

profitable and was well thought of within the newspaper community.

As a Christian, Dennis applied biblical standards of righteousness to the decisions he made in the marketplace. Some of those decisions related to advertisements. It's common for newspapers to reserve the right to advertise things they believe are constructive in the community and to withhold advertising for those things they believe are not helpful to their business or to the community at large. In light of that practice, Dennis eliminated advertisements for X-rated movies from the Dayton papers. He also refused to run notices and advertisements for gay and lesbian groups in the community.

As might be expected, that decision brought forth an outcry from the groups whose advertisements had been rejected. Yet Dennis remained committed to that which was righteous and true. The issue went to those in authority over him in Atlanta. Though they had backed him in similar decisions in the past, to his surprise they said he had to run the ads from the gay and lesbian groups or lose his job.

For Dennis, this was a trial of identification. He chose rather to identify with Christ than to continue in his career.

Hebrews 11:24–27 says of Moses:

> *By faith Moses, when he had grown up, refused to be known as the son of Pharaoh's daughter. He chose to be mistreated along with the people of God rather than to enjoy the pleasures of sin for a short time. He regarded disgrace for the sake of Christ as of greater value than the treasures of Egypt, because he was looking ahead to his reward. By faith he left Egypt, not fearing the king's anger; he persevered because he saw him who is invisible* (NIV).

To stand for Christ and His values in a hostile environment is bound to bring trials into our lives. As Christians, we must realize that throughout church history, the church has usually been planted in a hostile environment. In fact, rarely has the church thrived in a friendly context. More and more, there will be tests involving our identity with Jesus Christ.

In the midst of trials of identification, the pattern of success is to persist in righteousness, regardless of the cost. Peter wrote:

Dear friends, do not be surprised at the painful trial you are suffering, as though something strange were happening to you. But rejoice that you participate in the sufferings of Christ, so that you may be overjoyed when his glory is revealed. If you are insulted because of the name of Christ, you are blessed, for the Spirit of glory and of God rests on you. If you suffer, it should not be as a murderer or thief or any other kind of criminal, or even as a meddler. However, if you suffer as a Christian, do not be ashamed, but praise God that you bear that name (1 Peter 4:12–16 NIV).

Christians need to remain strong and demonstrate faithful perseverance in a test of identification.

> » **To stand for Christ and His values in a hostile environment is bound to bring trials into our lives.**

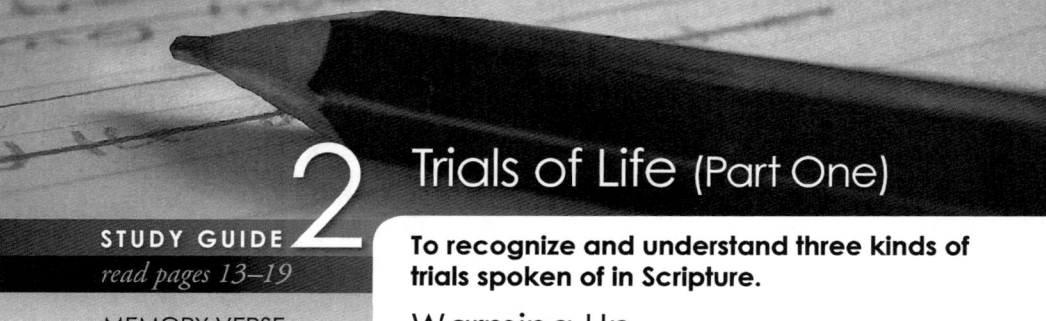

2 Trials of Life (Part One)

STUDY GUIDE
read pages 13–19

To recognize and understand three kinds of trials spoken of in Scripture.

MEMORY VERSE
2 Timothy 3:16—
"All Scripture is given by inspiration of God, and is profitable for doctrine, for reproof, for correction, for instruction in righteousness."

Warming Up

We all face the fallenness of humanity in differing ways. What are the most disturbing aspects to you of living in bodies that aren't perfect and in a society that is fraught with problems? _____

Thinking Through

1. Respond to the opening concept of the chapter: "We live in a fallen place. This planet is under the rule of our adversary, Satan." As believers in Jesus and as those who belong to the King of kings, how is that concept troubling? _____

2. What does Joe Stowell mean when he talks about "Trials of place and race" (pp. 13–15)? "Trials of temptation" (pp. 15–16)? "Trials of identification" (pp. 16–19)? _____

3. What does each kind of trial reveal about you? _____

Going Further

Refer

How can we respond biblically to each of the three kinds of trials?
Race and place (1 Peter 2:11–12, 20–24) _____

Temptation (Psalm 119:9–11) _____

Identification (1 Peter 4:12–16) _____

Digging In

Read 2 Corinthians 12:7–10

1. The apostle Paul wanted God to remove his "thorn in the flesh" (2 Corinthians 12:7). What do you think it was?

2. Why was the thorn given to Paul (v. 7)? Why didn't God take it away from Paul? What do you think of the idea that Paul lacked faith?

3. Knowing what we know about Paul and how he responded, what can we learn about handling an unwanted trial in our own lives?

⁷ And lest I should be exalted above measure by the abundance of the revelations, a thorn in the flesh was given to me, a messenger of Satan to buffet me, lest I be exalted above measure. ⁸ Concerning this thing I pleaded with the Lord three times that it might depart from me. ⁹ And He said to me, "My grace is sufficient for you, for My strength is made perfect in weakness." Therefore most gladly I will rather boast in my infirmities, that the power of Christ may rest upon me. ¹⁰ Therefore I take pleasure in infirmities, in reproaches, in needs, in persecutions, in distresses, for Christ's sake. For when I am weak, then I am strong.

Prayer Time

Use the *Our Daily Bread* article on the next page as a guide for a devotional and prayer time relating to the topic of trials.

Reflect

How has God used trials in your life to further His glory?

How have God's trials changed you?

How can it be possible, as J. B. Phillips says, not to "resent [trials] as intruders, but welcome them as friends"?

Our Daily Bread: For reflection & meditation about **trials**

When the Pressure Is On

What makes a shiny apple look so delicious? The skin, of course. But what is it about an apple that actually makes it delicious? The juice and substance inside. That's the apple's real "character."

I learned this as a boy watching my mom make applesauce. With a wooden pestle, she would mash the soft, boiled pieces of apple through a metal colander and into a bowl until all that remained in the colander were drab, flattened skins. But oh, the sauce tasted so good!

God uses life's pressures to bring out the sweetness of Christlike character in us. Tribulation (which means "pressure" in the Greek) also helps us realize the awful potential of our sin nature and see it for what it is—ugly and tasteless. Under pressure, all kinds of sins begin to surface —greed, selfishness, lust, pride.

Pressure, whether from without or from an unrealistic perfectionism within, is a fact of our fallen world. God controls its intensity and duration so that we can recognize, confess, and renounce those fleshly "skins" that obscure Christ's character in us.

Tribulation is not something anyone seeks. But when it comes, the Holy Spirit will use it to create in us perseverance, character, and hope (Romans 5:3–4).

—*Dennis De Haan*

ROMANS 5:3—
We also glory in tribulations, knowing that tribulation produces perseverance.

■ Read today's *Our Daily Bread* at **www.rbc.org/odb**

3

Trials of Life

PART TWO

Trials of Discipline

There are also trials of discipline. We need some clarification here. As noted earlier, not all difficulty in our lives is God's discipline. When difficulty affects us, we are prone to think that God is chastising us. That may not be true. We may be experiencing one of the trials we discussed earlier. But if it is discipline, it will be difficult. In discipline God seeks to nudge our lives back to paths of righteousness.

A VITAL DIFFERENCE

Note the difference between punishment and discipline.
- Punishment is justice.
- Discipline is corrective.

There is not one trouble that God brings into our lives as believers that is punishment. Sin was punished on the cross. We are not in double jeopardy. Every sin I have committed or will commit or am committing has been punished. Justice was meted out at the cross. But the corrective discipline of God comes along with sovereign nudges that inflict just enough pressure to alert me to the problem and get me back on track.

Proverbs 3:11–12 states, "My son, do not despise the Lord's discipline and do not resent his rebuke, because the Lord disciplines those he loves, as a father the son he delights in" (NIV). Hebrews 12 says that if you feel God disciplining you, rejoice. It's a sign of sonship. If He doesn't discipline you, you are not His child. I understand that kind of talk.

> ### ◼ FOCAL POINT
> Notice that in Hebrews 12:5, the writer prefaces the teaching about discipline by calling it a "word of encouragement" (NIV). What is encouraging about discipline?

I don't know how many times I've been in situations where I have wanted to put a little corrective pressure on someone else's child. But I had no right. The child was not my son or daughter. But with regard to my own children, not only do I have the right to "encourage" them into right paths when they get derailed but I also have the responsibility, the stewardship as a parent, to do just that.

How are we to respond to trials of discipline? By not resisting them. They come from a loving Father, and we need to open our hearts to these trials so that the Lord might correct us through them and put us on the right path.

THE EXAMPLE OF JONAH

There are many illustrations of this kind of trial in Scripture, but I can't resist going to the Old Testament prophet Jonah. The word of God came to the prophet: "Jonah, I want you to go to Nineveh." And he immediately said no. Here is the account of Jonah's journey.

> *Now the word of the Lord came to Jonah the son of Amittai, saying, "Arise, go to Ninevah, that great city, and cry out against it; for their wickedness has come up before Me." But Jonah arose to flee to Tarshish from the presence of the Lord. He went down to Joppa, and found a ship going to Tarshish; so he paid the fare, and went down to it, to go with them to Tarshish from the presence of the Lord.*
>
> *But the Lord sent out a great wind on the sea, and there was a mighty tempest on the sea, so that the ship was about to be broken up. Then the mariners were afraid; and every man cried out to his god, and threw the cargo that was in the ship into the sea, to lighten the load. But Jonah had gone down into the lowest parts of the ship, had lain down, and was fast asleep. So the captain came to him, and said to him, "What do you mean, sleeper? Arise, call on your God; perhaps your God will consider us, so that we may not perish." And they said to one another, "Come, let us cast lots, that we may know for whose cause this trouble has come upon us." So they cast lots, and the lot fell on Jonah. Then they said to him, "Please tell us! For whose cause is this trouble upon us? What is your occupation? And where do you come from? What is your country? And of what people are you? So he said to them, "I am a Hebrew; and I fear the Lord, the God of heaven, who made the sea and the dry land."*
>
> *Then the men were exceedingly afraid, and said to him, "Why have you done this?" For the men knew that he fled from the presence of the Lord, because he had told them. Then they said to him, "What shall we do to you that the sea may be calm for us?"—for the sea was growing more tempestuous. And he said to them, "Pick me up and throw me into the sea; then the sea will become calm for you. For I know that this great tempest is because of me." . . . So they picked up Jonah and threw him into the sea, and the sea ceased from its raging. . . .*
>
> *Now the Lord had prepared a great fish to swallow Jonah. And Jonah was in the belly of the fish three days and three nights (Jonah 1:1–17).*

■ FOCAL POINT

See the irony in Jonah's story? God's discipline sent him overboard during a storm and into the stinky innards of a fish. Dangerous as it was, it was what God used to get him on a "safe and successful" path, as Stowell puts it. Think of a time when you knew that God was disciplining you. While the path seemed rough, how did He prove to you that it was the best way to go?

What would God do? He needed somebody to go to Nineveh, but the prophet had just said he was not going—and was on his way somewhere else. In fact, Jonah was down in the hold of the ship, sound asleep. Discipline was God's response, sovereignly nudging Jonah back toward obedience—and Nineveh.

Some of us say to ourselves, *If I sin, I won't feel any peace. And I feel peace, so it must be all right.* Yet many times we have so rationalized our way into sin that we feel quite peaceful about it. Jonah's nap demonstrates that emotional peace is not a barometer of righteousness.

Jonah was so much at peace that he slept all the way through a storm. God had sent that storm to wake him up and bring him to his senses. But he kept sleeping. So God sent the captain of the ship down to see him. Sovereign nudge number two. The pagan ship captain shook Jonah and said, "Wake up! And pray to your God!" So Jonah got up and went to the deck of the ship. There the sailors were trying to find out who was responsible for their trouble.

They cast lots and gave everybody a number, including Jonah. As that ship tossed and turned under the delicate, sovereign hand of God, the lots were cast on the windswept deck—and wouldn't you know it, the lots pointed to Jonah. "Tell us," the sailors cried, "For whose cause is this trouble upon us? What is your occupation? And do you come from? What is your country? And of what people are you?" (v. 8).

He had to give a testimony. "He said to them, 'I am a Hebrew; and I fear the Lord, the God of heaven, who made the sea and the dry land' " (v. 9).

You'd think that by this time Jonah ought to be dropping to his knees—right? No. The trouble increased. "Then they said to him, 'What shall we do to you that the sea may be calm for us?' " (v. 11).

Jonah could have said, "I'll pray and repent, and your problem will be over." But Jonah replied, "Pick me up and throw me into the sea; then the sea will become calm for you. For I know that this great tempest is because of me" (v. 12). Jonah was saying, "I would rather die than obey God." Finally, in desperation, the sailors chucked him overboard. Now Jonah had won. God had nudged him and nudged him, and yet he had stubbornly maintained his sinful choice.

But when it comes to discipline, God has options we've never dreamed of. Just when Jonah thought he had won, God said to a great fish, "Do you see that boat? I want you to swim next to it, and when you see a splash, that's lunch." Jonah lived three days and three nights in that underwater hotel. He wrestled with God until finally, after three days of devastating discipline, he said, "God, You win."

When we sin, we can expect God to love us enough to keep working to bring us back to the course of righteousness. "The Lord disciplines those he loves" (Hebrews 12:6 NIV). And although this discipline is sometimes tough, He does it because He loves us enough to keep us on safe and successful paths.

Passing the test of discipline demands cooperation with God. When I was a boy, we used to like to wrestle to see whose young male ego could be affirmed. As little kids, we'd get a guy down, sit on top of him, and put him in a full nelson until he said one liberating word: "Uncle!"

That's how we respond to God. A trial of discipline is intended to get our stubborn wills to say, "All right! Uncle! I'm yours. I repent. I will gladly walk in righteousness."

Trials Of Consequence For Sin

There are also trials that are the consequence for sin. Chuck Swindoll says it so well: "We teach our children 1 John 1:9, 'If we confess our sins, He is faithful and just and will forgive us our sins and purify us from all unrighteousness,' which may tempt them to coast on grace." He goes on to say that "if we teach them 1 John 1:9, we must also teach them Galatians 6:8, 'The one who sows to please his sinful nature, from that nature will reap destruction' " (NIV).

Some of our trouble is a direct consequence of willful sin in our lives. Sin always brings consequences. Nobody is exempt. No one is clever enough, no one is subtle enough, no one is intelligent enough to sin and not bear its consequences. "Be self-controlled and alert. Your enemy the devil prowls around like a roaring lion looking for someone to devour" (1 Peter 5:8 NIV). In the Old Testament we read, "There is a way that seems right to a man, but its end is the way of death" (Proverbs 14:12). Sin always brings despair and trouble. Even long after we are forgiven, the consequences may remain. Some will not be removed until that final glorious day of redemption.

> **» Take heart. The consequence soon will pass.**

Paul, having murdered Christians, couldn't shake the memories. In the first chapter of 1 Timothy he calls himself the worst of sinners. Yet he used that consequence as a springboard to worship and praise.

Even though I was once a blasphemer and a persecutor and a violent man, I was shown mercy because I acted in ignorance and unbelief. The grace of our Lord was poured out on me abundantly, along with the faith and love that are in Christ Jesus. Here is a trustworthy saying that deserves full acceptance: Christ Jesus came into the world to save sinners—of whom I am the worst. But for that very reason I was shown mercy so that in me, the worst of sinners, Christ Jesus might display his unlimited patience as an example for those who would believe on him and receive eternal life (1 Timothy 1:13–17 NIV).

The troubling and sometimes lifelong consequences of sin ought to motivate and remind us of its awfulness so that we say, "God, this daily consequence

> ### ■ TIME OUT FOR THEOLOGY
>
> If we live in a fallen place and if we are part of a fallen race, how can we be held accountable for our errors? Do we really have a choice?

reminds me of Your amazing grace to love, forgive, forget, and receive me." It ought to be, as well, a protective shield to help us not to risk the path of sin again. And, significantly, it ought to make us take the focus of our hearts off this fleeting, fallen world and live for that grand and glorious day of redemption when all things will become new (Revelation 21:1–4).

First John 3:2 proclaims: "Dear friends, now we are children of God, and what we will be has not yet been made known. But we know that when he appears, we shall be like him, for we shall see him as he is" (NIV). I love this verse. Take heart. The consequence soon will pass. When He comes and we meet Him face to face, it will all be new. Consequences, even in our tears and brokenness, can result in praise and glory and a deepening love for God and His appearing instead of a heart soured and angry with Him.

3 Trials of Life (Part Two)

STUDY GUIDE
read pages 23–29

Understanding how believers in Christ are disciplined and how sin affects our lives.

MEMORY VERSE
Proverbs 3:11–12—
"My son, do not despise the chastening of the Lord, nor detest His correction; for whom the Lord loves He corrects."

Warming Up

This section sets forth a difference between punishment and discipline. Think of an example when a parent will teach his or her child using punishment. Using discipline. What is the difference? Do you agree that "punishment is justice, and discipline is corrective"?

Thinking Through

1. Joe Stowell says that when Christians sin, they are not punished by God (see p. 24). Why should Christians not be punished by God?

2. Stowell suggests that "passing the test of discipline demands cooperation with God" (p. 27). What steps ("sovereign nudges," Stowell calls them) did God go through with Jonah to nudge him back toward cooperation? (pp. 25–27).

3. How does Jonah's story illustrate that emotional peace is not a barometer of righteousness (pp. 26–27).

Going Further

Refer

Chuck Swindoll correctly notes that 1 John 1:9 could allow us to think we can "coast on grace." What does he mean? Romans 6:1–2 explains how faulty it is to do this. Paul says, "What shall we say then? Shall we continue to sin that grace may abound? Certainly not." In what ways might we be tempted to use grace as an excuse to do wrong?

Digging In   Read 1 Timothy 1:13–16

1. The apostle Paul was redeemed by Jesus, yet he continued to mention the after-effects of his pre-Christian sin (1 Timothy 1:13–16). What does this teach us about sin's ongoing impact?

2. Paul speaks of God's "longsuffering" (v. 16). What can that term help us see about ourselves and God's feeling toward us despite our sin?

¹³ I was formerly a blasphemer, a persecutor, and an insolent man; but I obtained mercy because I did it ignorantly in unbelief. ¹⁴ And the grace of our Lord was exceedingly abundant, with faith and love which are in Christ Jesus. ¹⁵ This is a faithful saying and worthy of all acceptance, that Christ Jesus came into the world to save sinners, of whom I am chief. ¹⁶ However, for this reason I obtained mercy, that in me first Jesus Christ might show all longsuffering, as a pattern to those who are going to believe on Him for everlasting life.

3. What do the words "I obtained mercy" mean for Paul (vv. 13, 16)? What is Paul saying about God's grace (v. 14) and the work of Christ here (v. 15)?

Prayer Time

Use the *Our Daily Bread* article on the next page as a guide for a devotional and meditation time relating the topic of trials.

Reflect

While Satan can't take our salvation from us, he still prowls around—eager to pounce and devour. What rationalizations lead Christians to give in to Satan?

Joe Stowell says that passing the test of discipline demands "cooperation with God." What must you do to cooperate with God?

Our Daily Bread: For reflection & meditation about **trials**

A Test of Faith

When I was a boy, I disliked the story of Abraham going to Mount Moriah to sacrifice his son Isaac. Why would God tell Abraham to do such a thing? I was an only son, and I didn't want that happening to me! My parents assured me that God was testing Abraham's faith. And he passed that test. Even with the knife in his hand, Abraham believed God (Genesis 22:8–10). He had learned that the Lord could be trusted.

It is easy to make a profession of faith. But the real test comes when God asks us to lay our dearest treasures on the line. As with Abraham, the issue becomes one of obedience. A businesswoman lost a high-paying job because she wouldn't compromise her standards. And a pastor was driven from his church when he obeyed God's Word and spoke out about racism in his congregation.

Shouldn't these people have been rewarded when they did the right thing? Faith meets its toughest test when we feel that the Lord has not rewarded our faithfulness.

You may be faced with giving back to God something you feel He has given you. Learn to see this test as an opportunity to demonstrate your faith in the One who always keeps His promises—even when you don't understand.

—*Haddon Robinson*

GENESIS 22:8— God will provide for Himself the lamb.

■ Read today's *Our Daily Bread* at **www.rbc.org/odb**

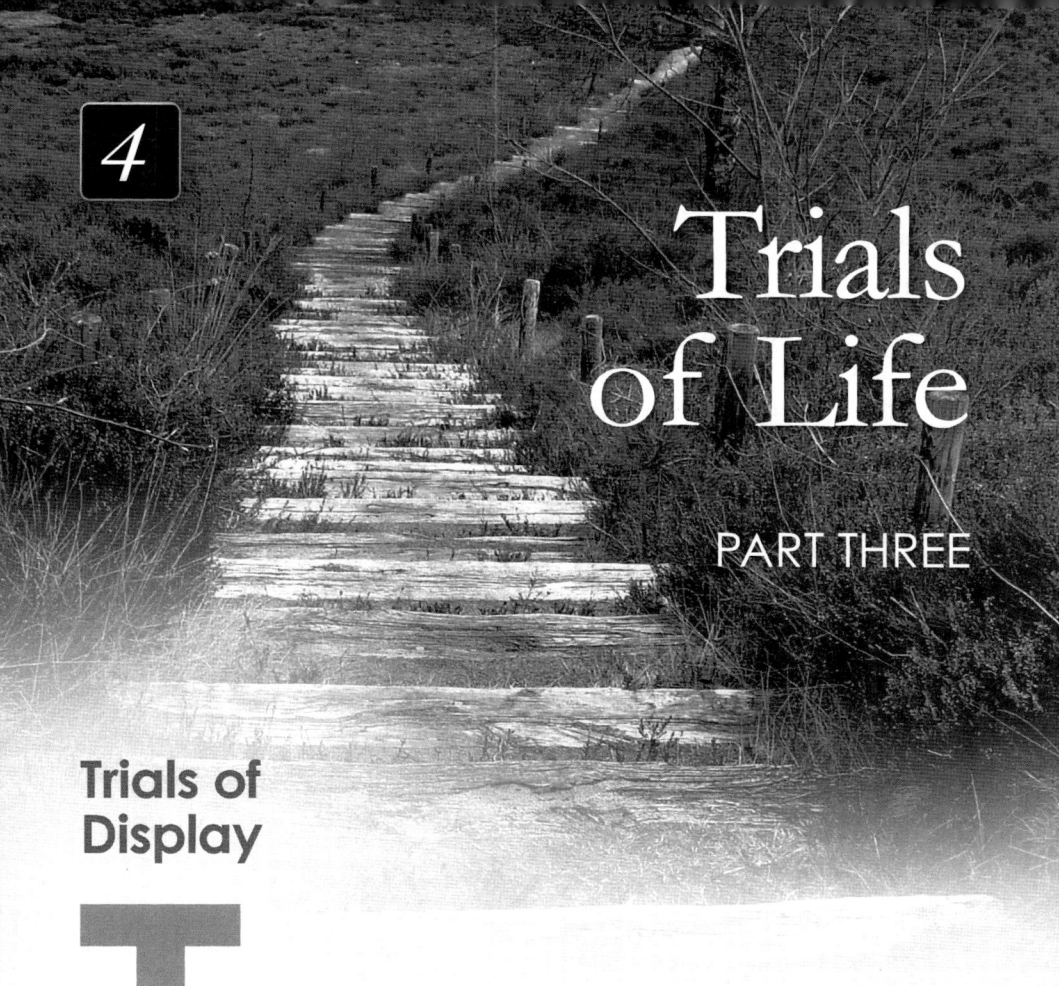

4

Trials of Life

PART THREE

Trials of Display

The sixth kind of trouble we might face is the trial of display. God permits this kind of trial to come into our lives to enable us to display something for Him through our trauma.

God came to Abraham and said, "Take now your son, your only son Isaac, whom you love, and go to the land of Moriah, and offer him there as a burnt offering on one of the mountains of which I shall tell you" (Genesis 22:2).

Quite frankly, when I hear that God asked for a child sacrifice, it troubles my spirit. I don't like to think that my God is like that. But we have to look at the context. In this particular instance, Abraham is living in the land of the Canaanites, where the highest form of commitment to their gods of wood and stone was taking their children and sacrificing them to their pagan god. Offering the blood of their children was the pinnacle statement of obedience to their god.

I believe that God was saying to Abraham, "Are you willing to display your love for Me, the true and the living God, as much as these pagans are to their gods?" I think there was something even more significant in this trial, this test in Abraham's life. Isaac was the gift God had given to Abraham. He was the miracle baby. Isaac was the whole reason Abraham left Ur of the Chaldees to become a pilgrim in the land of the Canaanites. Genesis 12:1–2, the passage that gives God's command to Abraham to leave Ur, is an early prophetic statement of the coming of Christ: "Now the Lord had said to Abram: 'Get out of your country, from your family and from your father's house, to a land that I will show you. I will make you a great nation; I will bless you and make your name great; and you shall be a blessing.'"

Years went by, and Abraham and Sarah were past childbearing age. Then suddenly, miraculously, God gave them the gift of this boy. Abraham loved Isaac.

I believe God was asking Abraham, "Do you love the gift more than the Giver?"

God often marches into our lives and threatens something precious to us—something He has given us. A child, a house, a spouse, a career. How do we respond? Do we display through our response that we love the Giver more than the gift?

> ### ■ FOCAL POINT
> What happens, though, when God goes beyond what Joe Stowell is suggesting? What happens when God actually allows something truly precious to be taken away? Is this still a trial of display? Abraham didn't lose a child, but we sometimes do. When tragedy strikes, how can we possibly still show that we "love the Giver more than the gift"?

I root for the Detroit Tigers and remain a loyal fan in good times and bad. During baseball season, every morning I open up the newspaper to see where the Tigers stand in the American League Central. God opens the newspaper of our lives to see whether He is still first or if something has displaced Him. Only you know. You may be asked to give that answer through a trial of display.

Abraham wakes up his boy on that morning, and they walk for three days. Abraham has a long time to change his mind, to flunk the test. He has three whole days of walking to say, "God, you're not first. Isaac is first in my life." And he walks three days, builds the altar, lays down his son—and now the marvelous statement of what kind of God our God is. God says, "Wait! That's all! That's all!" Genesis 22:12 puts it this way: "Do not lay a hand on the boy . . . . Do not do anything to him. Now I know that you fear God, because you have not withheld from me your son, your only son" (NIV).

Trials of display are intended to be a platform where God's power can be clearly seen. Such is the case with the man born blind (John 9:1–3).

As he went along, [Jesus] saw a man blind from birth. His disciples asked him, "Rabbi, who sinned, this man or his parents, that he was born blind?" "Neither this man nor his parents sinned," said Jesus, "but this happened so that the work of God might be displayed in his life" (NIV).

The blind man's trouble had nothing to do with the consequence of sin. His blindness was, instead, a platform upon which the glory and power of God could be seen. I often wonder what works of God are displayed in the midst of my trouble? Forgiveness, kindness, patience, grace? Or is my trouble a platform for Satan's agenda?

Trials Of Broken Expectation

The last kind of trial is the trial of broken expectations. You and I need to remember that one of the greatest difficulties we have in life is dealing with expectations that never come to pass. In fact, most counselors will tell you that much depression comes from the disappointment over broken expectations.

When we get married, we have expectations. A newly married husband expects a lot of things from his wife. And she has a whole list of expectations for him. He is expecting her to pick up after him, prepare wonderful meals, care for the brood, exhibit social graces, work like a strong bull at home, have the kids corralled, set a beautiful table with sterling candlesticks, have his favorite meal ready for him when he comes home, and after the meal—while he reads the paper—finish the work in the kitchen, put the kids to bed, and then be a tiger in the bedroom.

She has her list as well. He will be sensitive, understanding, and hang on every word uttered from her lips. He will keep her secure financially and spiritually, and she will always look at him as the rock of her life. He will help around the house and expect nothing of her when she is exhausted.

One of the great problems in marriage occurs when we realize that there is something wrong with those lists of expectations. That's when the trouble begins. None of us likes to have our dreams dashed.

On one occasion when our children were very small, they asked, "Dad, will you take us to the circus Tuesday night?" Not wanting to appear cruel and insensitive, I said, "Maybe." Which to their minds was yes. If you are a parent, or if you ever become one, know that anything short of an absolute, nonnegotiable, white-knuckled, teeth-clenched "NO!" is still a possibility. I said maybe and forgot about it.

I still remember coming home that Tuesday night. The kids were all excited. "Dad's home! Tonight's the night!"

"What's tonight?" I said.

"The circus! Remember?"

"Oh," I said, "we're not going to the circus."

They said, "Okay. No problem," and danced off merrily to do something else. Not a chance. They were crushed.

Broken expectations are a leading source of discouragement and despondency. The most instructive passage I know about expectations is in Philippians 1. It's the report that Paul files with the church in Philippi about his time in Rome. In this report he notes that he is imprisoned (v. 13), that some of the Roman believers are envious and spiteful toward him (v. 15), and that Nero may decree that his life be taken (vv. 19–24).

This has the makings for a lot of discouragement. What fascinates me is that in the midst of this trial of expectations, he is victorious and ecstatic. How? The answer is given in verse 20:

[It is] my earnest expectation and hope, that I will not be put to shame in anything, but that with all boldness, Christ will even now, as always, be exalted in my body, whether by life or by death (NASB).

Paul had one expectation in life. It wasn't to be the premier apostle. Nor was it to be well liked by brothers and sisters in Christ. It wasn't even to be given a longer life in which to serve Christ. Those were not his expectations. His one expectation was that Christ be magnified through him. He sought to demonstrate the quality, character, and agenda of Christ—regardless of his situation in life.

Rejecting comfort, pleasure, health, wealth, and peace as our primary expectations in life and instead placing the idea of reflecting Christ as our number one priority will not only direct us toward His glory but also help us bypass much trouble.

So, what can we expect from trouble? We can expect trouble to reveal ourselves as we really are and to come in at least seven different forms. And we can also expect trouble to elicit a response. The pivotal issue is what kind of response it will be.

4 Trials of Life (Part Three)

STUDY GUIDE
read pages 33–37

Understanding how God uses trials of display and broken expectations for His glory.

MEMORY VERSE
Philippians 1:20—
"According to my earnest expectation and hope that in nothing I shall be ashamed, but with all boldness, as always, so now also Christ will be magnified in my body, whether by life or by death."

Warming Up

Think of a situation in which your response to a negative life situation has had an impact—either good or bad—on other people.

Thinking Through

1. Put yourself in Abraham's shoes. You have been told that you are to sacrifice your only son on Mount Moriah. What is going through your mind as you trudge toward the mountain?

2. We usually think of this story as a display of Abraham's faithfulness, but Joe Stowell says it is a "marvelous statement of what kind of God our God is" (p. 35). What does this incident display to us about God?

3. Why are broken expectations a leading source of discouragement and despondency? In what ways are broken expectations good for us?

Going Further

Refer

Sometimes our expectation as Christians is that our faith will lead to a life of untroubled joy and happiness. How does Philippians 1:13–24 shed a different light on what we can expect as believers?

Digging In   Read   John 9:1–3

1. Upon seeing the blind man, why would the disciples ask Jesus such a question as "Who sinned, this man or his parents, that he was born blind?" (v. 2)?

> [1] Now as Jesus passed by, He saw a man who was blind from birth. [2] And His disciples asked Him, saying, "Rabbi, who sinned, this man or his parents, that he was born blind?" [3] Jesus answered, "Neither this man nor his parents sinned, but that the works of God should be revealed in him."

2. What was Jesus conveying to His listeners when He said, "Neither this man nor his parents sinned"?

3. Jesus was about to do a miracle in this man's life. Do you think the "works of God" (v. 3) are still displayed today in the form of miracles? Why or why not?

Prayer Time
Use the *Our Daily Bread* article on the next page as a guide for a devotional and meditation time relating to the topic of trials.

Reflect

Are you going through a trial of display? What purpose do you think God is trying to accomplish?

What trial of expectations has become an opportunity for God to demonstrate His power or glory? How has God used this trial to reveal himself and His glory to you?

Our Daily Bread: For reflection & meditation about **trials**

Expectations

Expectations! We all have them.

We expect that people will be nice to us, that we'll have good health, great marriages, faithful friends, successful careers. But what do we do when life doesn't live up to our expectations? In Philippians 1, Paul shows us the way. He faced broken expectations of place, people, and the future, yet he remained surprisingly upbeat.

Paul was stuck in prison—not a great place to be! When we get stuck in a tough marriage, an unrewarding job, or a challenging neighborhood, it's easy to get discouraged. But Paul was wonderfully positive. He said that his suffering helped to advance the gospel (Philippians 1:12).

Maybe people haven't lived up to our expectations. Paul likely expected other believers to encourage him. Instead, some were actually glad he was in jail and were preaching out of "envy and strife" (v. 15). Paul's response? "Christ is preached; and in this I rejoice" (v. 18).

Maybe it's an uncertain future—the loss of a spouse, a job transfer, or a health crisis. Paul knew that at any moment Nero might give the order for his execution, yet he declared, "For to me, to live is Christ, and to die is gain" (v. 21).

Adopt Paul's only expectation—for Christ to be honored no matter what!

—*Joe Stowell*

PHILIPPIANS 1:20—

My earnest expectation and hope [is] that… Christ will be magnified in my body, whether by life or by death.

■ Read today's *Our Daily Bread* at **www.rbc.org/odb**

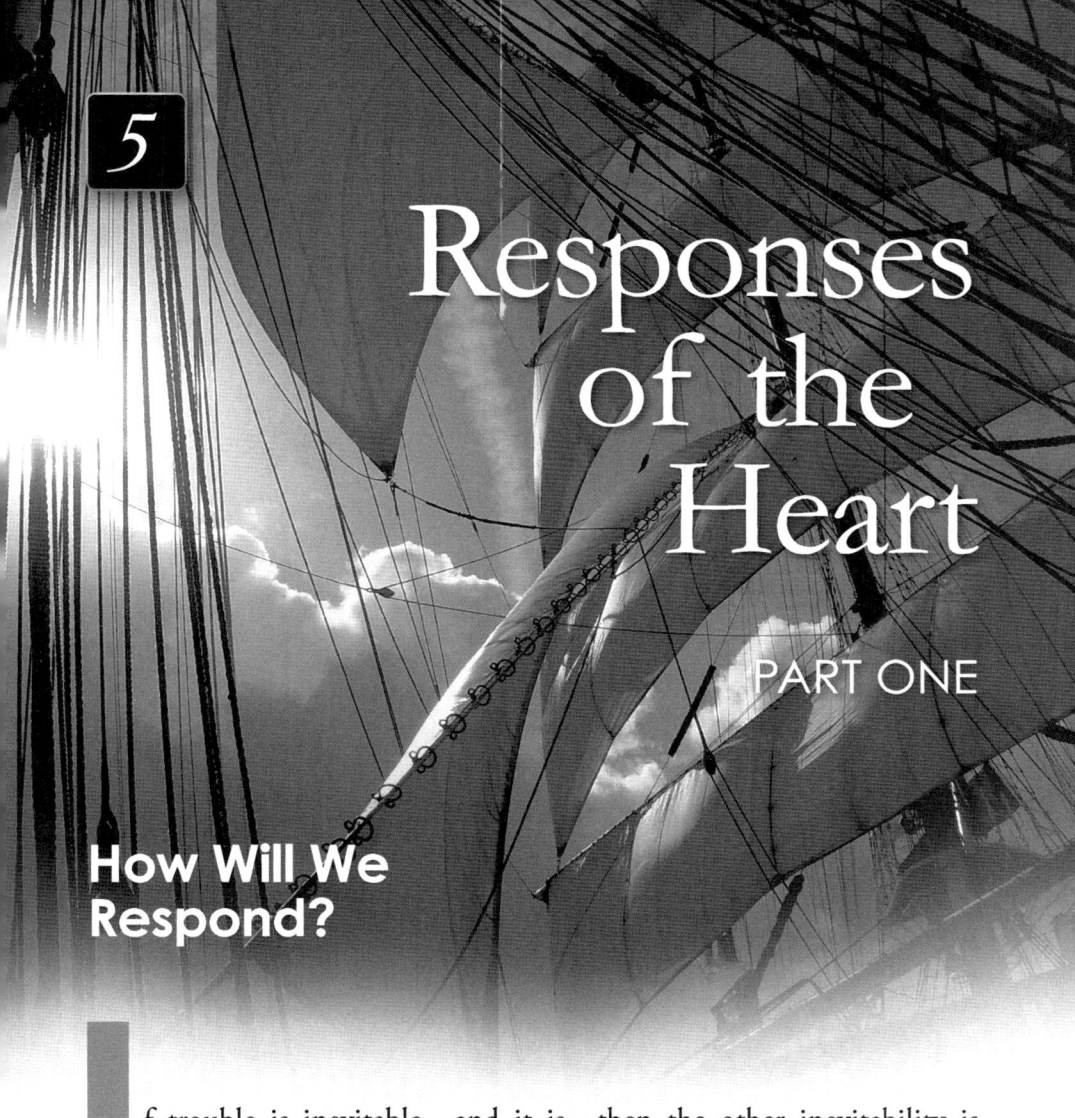

5

Responses of the Heart

PART ONE

How Will We Respond?

If trouble is inevitable—and it is—then the other inevitability is that we will indeed respond to it.

But how will we respond? We can respond passively, fearfully, inwardly, assertively, philosophically, manipulatively. When trouble interrupts us, there are a host of options.

Out of all the possible responses, one rises to the top. That strategic response is vital if we're to make it through. It is, in fact, nonnegotiable if we're to grow in character and competency and to bring glory to God's reputation.

The key is making a commitment to respond to trouble by "consider[ing] it pure joy" (James 1:2 NIV). Through our brokenness and tears, our hearts insist that this is impossible! Yet considering it pure joy is both possible and, when applied, productive. In fact, resisting this choice will derail progress and deepen despair.

Controlling Our Response

When James writes, "Consider it pure joy, my brothers, whenever you face trials of many kinds" (James 1:2 NIV), he is referring to an arena we can control. The timing, depth, complexity, and duration of trouble are for the most part beyond our control. However, we can control the way we respond.

An important goal in trouble is to respond in a way that minimizes long-term regrets. I recall standing by the casket with the parents of a son who had died in his twenties. I heard them say something that made a marked impression on my heart. They said, "We've not always been perfect parents, but we have no regrets. We enjoyed our life with him, and he enjoyed his relationship with us." What a wonderful commentary to come to the end of a relationship and to realize that while it wasn't perfect, there are no regrets.

The Result of a Right Response

Right responses in the midst of trouble always minimize regrets. One of the primary goals in moving through trouble successfully is to go through it in such a way that you can look back and realize that you did your best to respond properly and are not ashamed of how you managed the aspects that were in your control.

The story of Judas in Scripture is a fascinating and instructive illustration of a life of wrong responses that ended up in the depths of regret.

Because Judas was given the responsibility of being the treasurer for the disciples, it's obvious that he was trusted by them. So when Jesus said that one of the disciples seated at the table during the Last Supper would betray Him, it never occurred to anyone that He was referring to Judas. Even after Jesus clearly indicated the identity of His betrayer and told him to get on with his plan, none of the disciples understood whom Christ meant. They thought that when Judas left the room he was going to buy something for the Passover feast or give money to the poor (John 13:21–30).

> ### ■ FOCAL POINT
> For some, relationships unfortunately lead to regrets. When this is the case—when life doesn't turn out as we wish it would—how are we to respond?

Yet, in retrospect and under the inspiration of the Holy Spirit, John tells us that underneath it all, Judas was addicted to greed and personal gain and that indeed he was a thief. He would even steal from the treasury that he controlled (John 12:6). No doubt his dreams were that when Christ established His kingdom, he would be the treasurer and ultimately become a wealthy man.

Interestingly enough, it was right after Jesus announced that He was going to the cross and would not be establishing an earthly kingdom that Judas left the disciples and traded the head of Christ for money—thirty pieces of silver. It's as though he said to himself, "Now that my prospect of greater riches is gone, at least I can get thirty pieces of silver out of this deal."

What's significant is that Judas was more committed to his own comfort and ease than he was to going through difficulty in his identification with Christ, a trial that Christ predicted all the disciples would experience.

Judas' option for what seemed to be the comfortable way out was a response that filled the remainder of his life with regret, regret so deep that he couldn't live with himself. Matthew reports that after Judas betrayed Jesus and saw that "Jesus had been condemned," his heart was filled with sorrow (27:3).

Those thirty pieces of silver burned a hole in Judas' heart as they rattled in his bag. They became a symbol of his sorrow and a reminder of his regret. So deep was his regret that he went back to the Jewish leaders and threw the money at their feet. Then he went out and hanged himself. The response that had seemed the easiest, the most natural, and the most comfortable, that seemed to be exactly right and appropriate, ended up being the response that led Judas to the depths of despair.

As a pastor, I've been through several building programs. Of the things I've learned through that experience, number one is that you let the decorating committee do what it wants to do. It's much easier that way. In one of the churches I pastored, my secretary was bolder than I was. The committee thought we ought to have blue carpeting throughout the office complex. She did not like or want blue carpeting. She went head to head with the decorating committee over the issue and finally won. Her office would have beige, earth tones on the floor.

Just before the project was to be implemented, however, she walked into my office and said, "Pastor, I've decided to have blue carpeting in my office." I was shocked. She went on to say, "I realized last night that if I have my way on this carpeting, every time I walk into the office the carpet will be a reminder of my stubbornness."

> ### ■ FOCAL POINT
> Why is it that sometimes in our churches we create crises over silly things? Is it possible that we have become so self-centered that we don't even recognize the threat of regret? How can we avoid that in our church body?

Our response to a crisis will lead us either to reap a harvest of regrets that etch themselves on our minds as lifelong reminders of poor choices or to reap the joy of knowing that we chose the biblically correct response. Though the crisis may have been painful, we have the privilege of knowing that through it all we did our best—that our conscience is clear. Regardless of the outcome, we didn't do things that deepened our distress by accumulating symbols of sorrow through our sinful choices.

Productive responses are the responses that are outlined in God's Word. In times of crisis, we need to fight through the baggage of our feelings, instinctive responses, advice from well-meaning friends, and past response patterns to check in with God to see what He believes would be appropriate. Imagine being faced with a crisis and pausing—eyes glazed over a bit—only to hear someone ask, "What are you doing?" You respond, "Checking my biblical data bank to find out how to respond."

That's how the process begins.

PART ONE
Responses of the Heart

5

STUDY GUIDE
read pages 41–45

MEMORY VERSE
James 1:2–3—
"My brethren, count it all joy when you fall into various trials, knowing that the testing of your faith produces patience."

Seeing how we can learn right responses to life's trials.

Warming Up

Think about recent trials you have endured. What was a situation in which you handled the trial in a God-honoring way? What was a situation you wish you had handled better? What made the difference?

Thinking Through

1. Joe Stowell mentions a few ways we can choose to respond to trials: passively, fearfully, inwardly, assertively, philosophically, and manipulatively (p. 41). Which of these tends to be your default method for handling trials?

2. Why would you agree with Joe Stowell when he says, "Right responses in the midst of trouble always minimize regrets" (p. 42)? What would you deem to be the "right responses"? What are some regrets one might have from a wrong response?

3. Stowell says that "productive responses are the responses that are outlined in God's Word" (p. 45). What responsibilty does that imply for us? How do we increase our ability to respond rightly?

Going Further

Refer

Judas and Peter both failed Jesus during this time of testing. Both responded differently to their trials. Judas died in regret (Matthew 27:3–5), while Peter lived to become a great evangelist for Jesus. What are some differences between these two failures? Why did Peter survive his failure so well?

Digging In   Read   John 13:21, 25–30

> 21 When Jesus had said these things, He was troubled in spirit, and testified and said, "Most assuredly, I say to you, one of you will betray Me." 25 Then, leaning back on Jesus' breast, he said to Him, "Lord, who is it?" 26 Jesus answered, "It is he to whom I shall give a piece of bread when I have dipped it." And having dipped the bread, He gave it to Judas Iscariot, the son of Simon. 27 Now after the piece of bread, Satan entered him. Then Jesus said to him, "What you do, do quickly." 28 But no one at the table knew for what reason He said this to him. 29 For some thought, because Judas had the money box, that Jesus had said to him, "Buy those things we need for the feast," or that he should give something to the poor. 30 Having received the piece of bread, he then went out immediately. And it was night.

1. What major decision did Judas have to make (vv. 26–27)? What was the thing that Judas was to "do quickly" (v. 27)? Why didn't the other disciples suspect that the betrayer was Judas (vv. 28–29)?

2. What is the significance of the clause "Satan entered into him" (v. 27)? Is this something that can happen to Christians?

3. After Judas departed, after he did his evil deed, and after he was paid for his work, what happened with him (see Matthew 27:1–10)? What does Judas' horrible death indicate to us about facing a trial in a way that causes us to turn our back on God and experience regret?

Prayer Time

Use the *Our Daily Bread* article on the next page as a guide for a devotional and meditation time relating to the topic of trials.

Reflect

Have you (like Peter) ever been in such a fearful situation that you found it hard to speak the truth? What could help you to face such a trial without regrets?

Think of some times of crisis that ordinarily come to people you know. What items from your "biblical data bank" (p. 45) could come in handy in those kinds of situations?

Our Daily Bread: For reflection & meditation about **trials**

Choosing Joy

Most of us don't choose a difficult life—it chooses us. But we can choose our response to it. As someone once said, "Pain is inevitable but misery is optional." Yet, when difficulties arise, misery often seems to be the only option.

Author Lloyd Ogilvie tells of a Christian friend who was physically and emotionally depleted because of extreme pressures. A depressed mood engulfed him. When Ogilvie asked him how he was doing, he said grimly, "Well, joy's certainly no option!" Ogilvie replied, "You're right! Joy is no option. It's your responsibility."

Shocked, the friend retorted, "You talk about joy as if it were a duty." Ogilvie responded, "Right again!" He explained that we have a duty to God, ourselves, and others to overcome our moods and to battle through to joy.

In Romans 5, Paul gave these reasons for joy: We have peace with God through Christ, access into grace, and hope of future glory (vv. 1–2). We have assurance that tribulation produces perseverance, which in turn builds character and leads to hope (vv. 3–4). We have hope that doesn't disappoint, because God's love has been poured into our hearts (v. 5).

Fill your mind with these truths. Then, no matter what your circumstances, you can choose joy.

—*Joanie Yoder*

ROMANS 5:1—
Therefore, having been justified by faith, we have peace with God through our Lord Jesus Christ.

■ Read today's *Our Daily Bread* at **www.rbc.org/odb**

Responses of the Heart

The Joy of Our Response

PART TWO

How then should we respond? Although there are specific patterns of response relating to issues of forgiveness, compassion, mercy, understanding, justice, and patience, one general command fits every case. It is God's command to consider every trial to be a thing of joy.

Initially, that seems unreasonable, because trouble does not feel joyous. In fact, trouble and emotional joy are incompatible.

If we are to respond constructively, we must understand that James 1:2 does not tell us to feel joy. For that we can be thankful. It's impossible for us to manipulate our emotions. Emotions are a result of circumstances, body chemistry, how we have slept, what we have dreamed, or even what we may have eaten the night before. When I'm not feeling right about things, I don't have a joy button that I can press and suddenly feel wonderful. For the most part, emotions come and go and are often dictated by circumstances of life. And although we are usually able to keep our emotions in check, it's impossible to change them dramatically.

> ### ■ FOCAL POINT
> Seriously deal with this teaching by thinking about your natural objections to it. Clearly, it seems counterintuitive to apply joy to trials. How has this explanation helped you see the possibility of covering your difficulties with joy?

Emotions are the baggage that comes with our trouble. They were never intended to direct our response. They come along for the ride. The emotions we feel are legitimate and normal. Feeling guilty about feeling down is unnecessary and wrong. Even Jesus wept.

What's right, however, is that we can't permit our feelings to dictate how we respond. If you have traveled through the mountains, you may have seen ramps for runaway trucks. They are for drivers who have lost their brakes and are dangerously careening down the road out of control. At that point, their trucks are driven by the weight of their baggage. It's a disaster waiting to happen. Letting our emotions dictate our actions is like letting the baggage do the driving.

It's in our choices that our lives should be directed to a productive end. When we understand what the word *consider* means, it becomes clear that James is speaking of a nonemotional choice in this text. Among other things, the word *consider* is an accounting term for "reckoning items one to another." In fact, some Scripture versions use the word *reckon* in the place of *consider*. At any rate, it's clearly a word that deals with cognitive, mental, volitional activity as opposed to emotional feelings. The text requires that when pain penetrates my existence I need to immediately, mentally, reckon that pain to be a thing of ultimate joy.

Since in the original language the word *consider* is used in accounting contexts, we can think of our minds as a ledger book with different columns we can use to record our response when difficulty crosses our path. Our response to difficulty might be to pick up the pencil of our mental notebook and put a check in the self-pity column, wondering why this is happening again and why we're always having difficulty. So we throw a pity party for ourselves and wallow in the despair of "woe is me." That's one type of mental response.

There's another column that is often checked—the column of blame. We might try to figure out who is to blame for our problem (of course we never are) and put a check in the blame column, as we seek to put off any feelings of personal responsibility for the mess we're in.

Or we may put a check in the column of revenge. I'm amazed at how creative we can be when it comes to carrying out revenge against others who have hurt us. There's a column for withdrawal. There is a life-is-unfair column. There are columns for bitterness and guilt. But there's also a column for joy. Scripture demands that we move all the way across the ledger page until we come to the column labeled joy and mentally make a checkmark indicating our belief that, in the hand of God, what has happened will ultimately be a cause for joy.

The Content of Our Response

James 1:2–5 points to the fact that this is not simple mental gymnastics or the power of positive thinking to get us through. This "joy" response has real content.

The end of the passage makes it clear that if we process pain correctly, it will, in the end, bring us to completion in terms of character and equip us to be completed in good works in the ongoing days of our lives. God will use our trouble to produce character and competency in our lives. That is the joy factor.

We should notice what the author of Hebrews says of Jesus and His suffering: *"Looking unto Jesus, . . . who for the joy that was set before Him endured the cross" (12:2).*

Counting trouble a thing of joy does not require that we feel happy about our difficulties but that we understand that ultimately and finally God's

≫ We can know that pain is a process with a purpose.

good hand will make the experience worthy of joyful praise and thanksgiving. This mental outlook keeps our focus not on the moment of pain but on the culmination of the process.

What enables us to respond positively? The joy response is fortified by what we know to be true in the midst of trouble.

James 1:3 speaks to the process of the joy response by saying, "because you know" (NIV). That statement directly ties our ability to count our difficulty an ultimate thing of joy to what we know to be absolutely true. There is a tremendous advantage believers have when they face trouble by depending on the truths that are logged in their mind before the trouble comes.

There are times when trouble puts us in such deep despair that our capacity to learn through it is almost nonexistent. Logging the right kind of knowledge in advance is greatly beneficial in light of the inevitability of tough times in our lives.

The success of the Persian Gulf War is likely attributable to the fact that the allied pilots were well trained before they actually faced battle. As one military commander observed, the generation raised on video games was able to take control of sophisticated equipment that required good eye-hand coordination and accurate timing. When the conflict came, they were well prepared in the skills it required.

Knowledge, whether learned in the midst of trouble or logged in advance, is that commodity that remains certain in the midst of changing emotions and circumstances. It's like an anchor firmly secured in bedrock that keeps the storm-tossed ship from being blown onto rocks.

One of my all-time favorite sports memories is one of the final hockey games played in the 1980 Winter Olympics in Lake Placid, New York. The American team, made up for the most part of amateur players from colleges and universities, was facing Scandinavian and Eastern Bloc teams composed of seasoned veterans who had given their lives to the state to prepare for and to compete in the Olympic contests. The Americans seemed to be outmatched. And because the Olympics came at a time when the spirit of Americans was at an all-time low, there was little to cheer about.

Yet the American team persisted and won game after game. On the day the US team was playing the dominant Russian team, I came home and turned the television on and noted, much to my surprise, that though the match was more than half over, we were playing head to head with them. I sat down and could hardly move. I watched with anxiety as our men skated, and I flinched every time the Russians cocked their sticks to take a shot. I relaxed in relief each time they didn't score. It was an agonizing, white-knuckle, tight-stomach spectator event for me and for many others who watched across the country.

Then, in the final moments, it became obvious that we would beat the Russians. It seemed impossible. It seemed so wonderful. We at last had something to cheer about. We had done it.

A few days later, the network decided to replay the hockey game. So we invited some friends over to enjoy it with us. I sat back in my easy chair, a glass of Pepsi in my hand and a bowl of popcorn on my lap. I was relaxed, calm, and enjoying every moment of the very same game—no whitened knuckles, no tight stomach. What made the difference? What I knew. What I knew to be true! The outcome was secure.

What we know to be true, regardless of the specific trouble we are going through, is the foundation upon which we can accurately, reasonably, intelligently, and confidently go to the joy column on our ledger page and put a check in the appropriate place.

What is it that we can know to enable us to respond positively in trouble? In James 1:3–4, we are told that we can know "that the testing of [our] faith develops perseverance" and that "perseverance must finish its work so that [we] may be mature and complete, not lacking anything" (NIV). In other words, we can know that pain is a process with a purpose. And that specific piece of knowledge will enable us to respond to our various trials with joy.

PART TWO
Responses of the Heart

STUDY GUIDE 6
read pages 49–53

Discovering joy as the end result of your trials.

MEMORY VERSE
Hebrews 12:2—
"Looking unto Jesus, the author and finisher of our faith, who for the joy that was set before Him endured the cross."

Warming Up

List ten things that have happened to you in the past year. Categorize them into "Happy Events," "Unhappy Events," and "Joyful Events." What is a "happy event" for you? "Joyful"? What's the difference? _____

Thinking Through

1. James 1:2 tells us to "consider it pure joy" when we face trials. What is the distinction between doing that and having "emotional joy" (p. 49)? _____

2. Joe Stowell suggests that we understand the word *consider* in verse 2 as an accounting term (p. 50). He mentions several ledger columns we can use to categorize our trials. What are those columns, and what others have you found yourself or others using? In what way does the "joy" column trump all the others? _____

3. On page 52, we read this: "What enables us to respond positively? The joy response is fortified by what we know to be true in the midst of trouble." What are some things you know for sure—things that help you keep the right perspective when difficulties come into your life? _____

Going Further

Refer

Hebrews 12 explains that Jesus went through a huge trial—yet He did it "for the joy" (v. 2). Think of the contrast between Jesus' agony in Gethsemane as He contemplated the cross (Matthew 26:36–46) and the joy He experienced in knowing what His pain would provide (Hebrews 12:2). The verse mentions the "throne of God." Imagine Jesus' joy as He sees from His throne all who are joining Him because of His sacrifice. Discuss this concept.

Digging In Read James 1:2–6

1. Is James telling us to count our joys or to count our trials (v. 2)? What does it mean to "count it all joy when you fall into various trials"?

2. How is a trial "the testing of your faith" (v. 3)? What is God's desired outcome of our trials (v. 4)? How does knowing God's purpose for our trials help us respond correctly to them?

3. If we are having trouble understanding how this works, we have a resource. What is it (vv. 5–6)? What does this whole process teach us about God?

> [2] My brethren, count it all joy when you fall into various trials, [3] knowing that the testing of your faith produces patience. [4] But let patience have its perfect work, that you may be perfect and complete, lacking nothing. [5] If any of you lacks wisdom, let him ask of God, who gives to all liberally and without reproach, and it will be given to him. [6] But let him ask in faith, with no doubting, for he who doubts is like a wave of the sea driven and tossed by the wind.

Prayer Time

Use the *Our Daily Bread* article on the next page as a guide for a devotional and meditation time relating to the topic of trials.

Reflect

If we begin to "grow weary and lose heart" because of our trials, Hebrews 12:2 tells us to think about Jesus. How can His joy help us place a check in the "joy" column (p. 51–52)?

Write down all the troubles facing you. Thank God for each of them. Then give them over to Him.

Our Daily Bread: For reflection & meditation about **trials**

Wall-Bangers Anonymous

I'll never forget the time during college when, after I had finished writing a big paper that was due the next day, I heard a loud commotion in the room across the hall. My neighbor was in a state of panic, throwing stuff around his room looking for his paper. Frustrated, he banged his fist against the wall and shouted, "Thanks a lot, God. You make life one big laugh!"

I might have given him an A+ for theology—at least he knew that God was ultimately in charge—but an F for his response to the problem.

For those of us who get mad at God when life takes a wrong turn, we need a good dose of biblical therapy. So, welcome to "Wall-Bangers Anonymous"—a two-step program toward a positive, God-honoring response to pain.

Step One: Think straight about trouble. It's not only inevitable, it's indiscriminate. Trouble comes in all shapes and sizes. "Various trials" (James 1:2) affect our health, our careers, our relationships. Once we understand the facts, we can begin appreciating their significant value in our lives.

Step Two: Trade resistance and resentment for receptivity and rejoicing. "Count it all joy" (v. 2). The joy is not in the presence of pain but in the knowledge that God is using our pain to refine us and make us better, not bitter.

—*Joe Stowell*

JAMES 1:2—

My brethren, count it all joy when you fall into various trials.

■ Read today's *Our Daily Bread* at **www.rbc.org/odb**

LEADER'S and USER'S GUIDE

Overview of Lessons

STUDY	TOPIC	BIBLE TEXT	READING	QUESTIONS
1	Understanding Our Trials	1 Peter 1:5–9	pp. 6–9	pp. 10–11
2	Trials of Life (Part One)	2 Corinthians 12:7–10	pp. 13–19	pp. 20–21
3	Trials of Life (Part Two)	1 Timothy 1:13–16	pp. 23–29	pp. 30–31
4	Trials of Life (Part Three)	John 9:1–3	pp. 33–37	pp. 38–39
5	Responses of the Heart (Part One)	John 13:21, 25–30	pp. 41–45	pp. 46–47
6	Responses of the Heart (Part Two)	James 1:2–6	pp. 49–53	pp. 54–55

Pulpit Sermon Series (for pastors and church leaders)

Although the Discovery Series Bible Study is primarily for personal and group study, pastors may want to use this material as the foundation for a series of messages on this important issue. The suggested topics and their corresponding texts from the Overview of Lessons above can be used as an outline for a sermon series.

DSBS User's Guide (for individuals and small groups)

Individuals—Personal Study
- Read the designated pages of the book.
- Carefully consider the study questions, and write out answers for each.

Small Groups—Bible—Study Discussion
- To maximize the value of the time spent together, each member should do the lesson work prior to the group meeting.
- Recommended discussion time: 45 minutes.
- Engage the group in a discussion of the questions—seeking full participation from each member.

Note To The Reader

The publisher invites you to share your response to the message of this book by writing Discovery House Publishers, P.O. Box 3566, Grand Rapids, MI 49501, USA. For information about other Discovery House books, music, videos, or DVDs, contact us at the same address or call 1–800–653–8333. Find us on the Internet at **http://www.dhp.org/** or send e-mail to **books@dhp.org**.